CONTENTS

A BIG PUSH 4

HEADING FOR WAR 6

THE BATTLE RAGES 10

LIFE IN THE TRENCHES 18

WAR ACROSS THE WORLD 24

INDUSTRIAL WAR 28

BEGINNING OF THE END 36

TIMELINE 42

FIND OUT MORE 44

GLOSSARY 46

INDEX 48

Any words appearing in the text in bold, **like this**, are explained in the glossary. You can also look out for them in the Word Bank box at the bottom of each page.

A BIG PUSH

The Great War

World War I began in 1914 and ended in 1918. It was the first war that involved many different countries all across the world, and so became known as the "Great War". More than eight million soldiers died during the war.

In September 1915, Patrick MacGill was a soldier in the British army, near Loos in France. There was going to be a "big push" to attack the German **lines** in the area. Patrick carried stretchers. It was his job to help soldiers who were wounded in battle.

British big guns pounded the German lines for four days, trying to destroy their defences. At 6.30 a.m. on 25 September, the British soldiers climbed out of their **trenches** and moved "**over the top**" towards the Germans. Patrick followed another soldier up a ladder. The soldier was killed by a bullet in the head. Patrick had to climb over the body to get to the top.

These British troops are leaving the safety of their trenches to go "over the top" to face the terror of enemy gunfire. A shell explodes to their right. ➡

Word Bank   morphine   strong medicine given to reduce pain
no-man's land   unclaimed area of land separating enemies

On the Front Line

IN THE TRENCHES IN WORLD WAR I

Adam Hibbert

www.raintreepublishers.co.uk
Visit our website to find out more information about **Raintree** books.

To order:
☎ Phone 44 (0) 1865 888113
🖹 Send a fax to 44 (0) 1865 314091
🖳 Visit the Raintree Bookshop at **www.raintreepublishers.co.uk** to browse our catalogue and order online.

Produced for Raintree by
White-Thomson Publishing Ltd,
Bridgewater Business Centre,
210 High Street, Lewes, BN7 2NH

First published in Great Britain by Raintree,
Halley Court, Jordan Hill, Oxford OX2 8EJ,
part of Harcourt Education.
Raintree is a registered trademark of
Harcourt Education Ltd.

Editorial: Juliet Smith and Daniel Nunn
Design: Michelle Lisseter and Clare Nicholas
Picture research: Amy Sparks
Project manager: Juliet Smith
Production: Duncan Gilbert

Originated by Dot Gradations Ltd
Printed and bound in China by South China
Printing Company Ltd

ISBN 1 844 43689 6
09 08 07 06 05
10 9 8 7 6 5 4 3 2 1

**British Library Cataloguing in
Publication Data**
Hibbert, Adam 1968–
In the Trenches in World War I. – (On the Front Line)
1. World War, 1914–1918 – Campaigns – Juvenile
literature
I. Title
940.4'14
A full catalogue record for this book is
available from the British Library.

Acknowledgements
The publishers would like to thank the following for
permission to reproduce photographs:
AKG pp. **14–15**, **16**, **17**(r), **24**(r), **32**, **36**, **38**(b);
Corbis pp. **13**, **14**(l), **15**(r), **21**, **26**, **27**, **31**, **33**, **40**;
Harcourt pp. **title page**, **4–5**, **7**, **8**, **12**(l), **20**, **23**(r),
34–35, **37**(t), **37**(b), **38**(t); Popperfoto p. **18**; Topfoto pp.
9, **11**, **12**(r), **17**(l), **19**(l), **19**(r), **24**(l), **25**, **28**(l), **28–29**,
30, **35**, **39**, **41**. Cover photograph of soldiers of the Royal
Irish Rifles in the trenches during the Battle of the
Somme in 1916, reproduced with permission of AKG.

Maps on pp. 6, 10 by Peter Bull.

Source notes: p. **13** quote from *The Private Papers of
Douglas Haig, 1914–1919* (Eyre and Spottiswood, 1952);
p. **14** quote from *Everyman at War: Sixty personal
narratives of the War* (J. M. Dent & Sons, 1930); p. **20**
quote from *Four Weeks in the Trenches: The War Story of a
Violinist* (Gutenberg.org #10967, 2004); p. **29** extract
from *Wilfred Owen, 1917, in Poems*, introduced by
Siegfried Sassoon (Chatto & Windus, 1920); p. **33** quote
from *Pillows of Fire: The Battle of Messines Ridge, June
1917* (Sutton Publishing, 2004).

Every effort has been made to contact copyright holders
of any material reproduced in this book. Any omissions
will be rectified in subsequent printings if notice is given
to the publishers.

The paper used to print this book comes from
sustainable resources.

Death in no-man's land

Patrick could not believe his eyes as he crossed **no-man's land**. Through bullets, smoke, and poisonous gas, soldiers walked slowly towards the German trenches. Wounded men crawled back towards their own lines, or sat huddled, in shock. Parts of bodies – legs and arms – lay all over the ground.

Patrick could not do much to help his wounded comrades except offer a bandage and a **morphine** pill to reduce the pain. The poison gas made him feel dizzy, and even made the situation seem funny for a second. By nightfall, Patrick had lost count of the number of dying men he had cared for. Within three days, the Germans drove British survivors back to their starting point. The "big push" was over.

Find out later

Why were trenches built in a zig-zag design?

What is the name of the German soldier on the right?

How did the Germans use dogs like this in the trenches?

"over the top" phrase used to describe climbing out of a trench and moving into battle

HEADING FOR WAR

Battleships

In the early 1900s, Germany began building a High Seas **Fleet** to compete with Britain's Grand Fleet. This made many people in Britain suspect that Germany was looking for a fight.

At the start of the 20th century, there were four powerful nations in Europe: Britain, France, Germany, and Russia. These are sometimes called the "powers". Germany was a new country, created out of smaller states in 1871. France and Russia were powerful old countries. Britain controlled the seas with its battleships. All these countries competed with each other to control **resources** and trade. Some British leaders called this competition "the Great Game".

Britain, France, and Russia each controlled **territories** around the world. Their military strength helped them to persuade smaller countries everywhere to take their side in "the Great Game". Germany had grown rich and powerful after 1871, but did not have many territories overseas. This meant that Britain, France, and Russia were able to stop Germany winning control of resources.

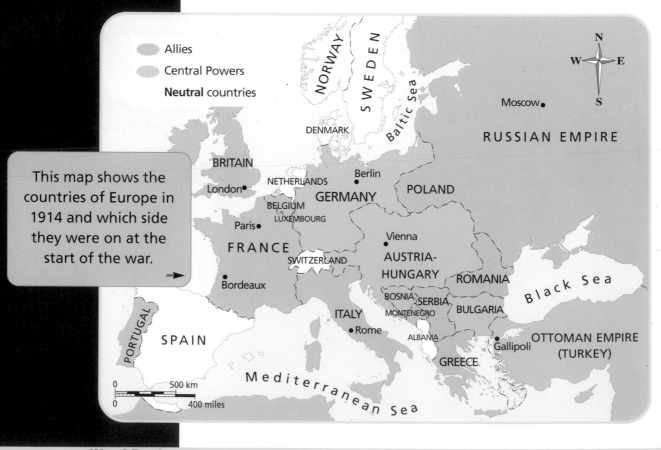

This map shows the countries of Europe in 1914 and which side they were on at the start of the war. →

Word Bank   **fleet**   group of warships, or an entire navy
resources   useful materials, such as oil or metals

6

Promises

In 1839, Britain had promised to defend Belgium, a small country between Germany and France, if it was attacked. This promise was a warning to France and Germany. If either one attacked the other through Belgium, Britain would become their enemy. France and Russia also promised to help each other if Germany attacked either of them. Germany made a similar agreement with its neighbour, **Austria-Hungary**. All these promises had an important effect. If any one of these nations started a war, all the European powers would have a reason to join in.

War fever

People in Europe had been expecting war for many years. Millions celebrated when war started, and tens of thousands of young men immediately rushed to join their country's army. The crowds in the photograph below are celebrating the start of World War I outside Buckingham Palace in London.

territories   areas of land belonging to one country

Reasons for war

There were many reasons why World War I began, including:

- countries competing for rich **resources**
- national pride
- lots of different countries agreeing to help each other
- the murder of Franz Ferdinand
- many mistakes made by leaders.

The first shot

The event that is blamed for starting World War I happened on 28 June 1914 when a man called Archduke Franz Ferdinand was murdered. He was the next in line to be emperor of **Austria-Hungary**. The killer, Gavril Princip, belonged to a terrorist group from Serbia. On 23 July, Austria-Hungary threatened to invade Serbia to punish the killers. But Serbia was a friend of Russia. Austria-Hungary's threat caused Russia to prepare its army for action. Russia's move also forced Germany and France to prepare their armies.

Leaders across Europe expected the crisis to calm down. The **Kaiser** of Germany (Wilhelm II) and the **Tsar** of Russia were cousins. It was thought that royal families would not fight against each other. But the nations of Europe seemed ready for a war, regardless of how individual leaders felt.

Archduke Franz Ferdinand and his wife, seated in the back of the car, minutes before they were assassinated. →

Word Bank   Kaiser   name used for the rulers of Austria-Hungary and Germany

The Schlieffen Plan

There was another problem. Germany's secret plan for war was made by the Chief of the German general staff, Alfred Graf von Schlieffen, in 1905. It looked like Germany's only chance to beat France, to the west, and Russia, to the east. Schlieffen's plan was a surprise attack through Belgium behind the French army and on to Paris, the capital of France. Germany might be able to defeat France before Russia was ready to fight. Then the whole German army would be free to fight Russia.

However, Russia was already preparing for war in 1914, so Germany's only chance of victory was slipping away. Waiting for peace talks would leave Germany defenceless. So, on 4 August 1914, German troops swept into Belgium, aiming for France.

Armed strength

By 1914, countries all over the world had thousands of soldiers ready to fight.

Germany	850,000
Austria-Hungary	430,000
France	750,000
Russia	1,500,000
Britain	120,000
British Empire	170,000
Belgium	43,000
Japan	75,000
United States	25,000

Kaiser Wilhelm II (in front of the flag) receives a report on troop movements before the outbreak of war in 1914.

Tsar   name used for the rulers of Russia

THE BATTLE RAGES

Flanking

It is hard to attack an army head on. In battle, soldiers always look for a way to attack from the side or from behind. This is called flanking. Part of the Schlieffen Plan was based on the German army flanking the whole of the French army.

Once they had launched their attack, German troops soon blasted past the Belgian army and into northern France. The Schlieffen Plan was working, and in no time the German army was marching towards Paris. The battle areas of France and Belgium became known as the **Western Front**. Four British **infantry divisions** (about 80,000 men), called the British Expeditionary Force (BEF), joined the French to fight against the Germans.

Rapid advance

Despite the news from Belgium, France and Britain (called the "**Allies**") were still caught by surprise. They were soon forced back by the Germans. With the Germans just 50 kilometres (30 miles) from Paris, the French government quickly moved to Bordeaux in the south of France. But the German army had moved so quickly that the soldiers lost contact with their headquarters, food supplies, and spare troops. This weakened the German army and gave the Allies a chance to recover.

This map shows how far the Germans advanced in 1914. It also shows the location of the Western Front for most of the war between 1914 and 1916.

Word Bank   **Allies** countries such as the United Kingdom, France, the United States, and Russia that fought together against Germany

Battle of the Marne

On 6 September 1914, the Allies fought back near the River Marne in France. The Battle of the Marne split the German army into two parts, leaving it open to great danger. Three days later, on 9 September, the German commander ordered his army to **retreat**.

A line of trenches

The Germans began to dig defensive **trenches**. The Allies tried to move past the trenches to surround them. This forced the German army to spread their trenches sideways. A very long line of trenches sprang up all the way along the battlefront. By Christmas it was 800 kilometres (500 miles) long, running from the sea in the north to the mountain border with Switzerland in the south.

No-man's land

When two enemy armies dug trenches to shelter in, there was a space between them that neither side controlled. This was called "**no-man's land**". It was a dangerous place, exposed to gunfire, full of big holes made by the explosions of shells and bombs, and surrounded by barbed wire.

These troops from New Zealand have dug into a trench in northern France.

retreat   move back
Western Front   battlefront between Germany and France

The world sends troops

Nelson and Frederic Scrivener lived in Queensland, Australia. Like many other men throughout the **British Empire**, they were eager to help Britain in the war. In 1914, at only twenty years old, Nelson was too young to **volunteer** without his parents' permission. So Nelson pretended he was 23 and joined the Australian army, together with his brother Fred. They set sail for Europe on 24 September 1914.

After two months, the brothers discovered that their ship was not going to Europe. The British army was too busy training British volunteers to cope with more people from other countries. They went to Egypt instead, landing in time for Christmas. But, after only two months in Egypt, new orders were issued. The brothers would be fighting in the Mediterranean against Germany's ally, the **Ottoman Empire**.

Sailing to the trenches

Many countries sent troops to fight alongside the **Allies** already involved in the war. These included:

Countries	Soldiers
Australia	322,000
Canada	418,000
India	70,000
New Zealand	100,000
South Africa	33,000

The poster on the near right was used to encourage young men in Britain to join the army. The poster on the far right appealed to men across the British Empire to join the war. →

BRITONS "WANTS" YOU JOIN YOUR COUNTRY'S ARMY! GOD SAVE THE KING

THE EMPIRE NEEDS MEN

THE OVERSEAS STATES All answer the call. Helped by the YOUNG LIONS The OLD LION defies his Foes ENLIST NOW.

Word Bank   volunteer   join something of one's own free will

Nelson and Fred were sent to Lemnos, a Greek island in the Mediterranean. They had only seven weeks to train with the rest of the army that was gathering there from Asia and the Pacific.

Brothers into battle

At the end of April 1915, the campaign to attack the Ottoman Empire began with the assault on Gallipoli (see page 26). Although the brothers wanted to stay together, Nelson was hit by a bullet in the leg as they scrambled from boats onto the beach, and was sent to hospital. Fred stayed on to carry stretchers and to help the wounded. Both brothers survived the war.

Keen to help

After reviewing Australian troops as they arrived in France in March 1916, the British commander, Douglas Haig, wrote in his diary:

"The Australians are mad keen to kill Germans and to start doing it at once!"

This huge crowd of people has gathered on Melbourne docks to say goodbye to Australian troops leaving for the war in Europe.

This German trench and **bunker** near Verdun in France can still be visited today. You can see how the trench zig-zags.

Trench design

On the **Western Front**, the British, French, and German armies were digging in. Simple **trenches** soon became complex underground "cities". Both sides dug networks of trenches that could shelter an entire army.

Trenches were usually deeper than a tall man. A well-built trench had sides propped up with logs. To fire a rifle over the front edge of the trench, soldiers would step onto a ledge in the front wall, called a "fire step". Where the ground was too hard or wet for digging, they piled sandbags up instead. The front trench would be built in a zig-zagged line along the battlefront. This was so that if enemy soldiers captured it, they could not shoot along it.

Gruesome signposts

A. A. Dickson, a British officer in the Sherwood Foresters, remembers how soldiers would use body parts to find their way through the battlefield.

"We learned the landmarks to guide us: 'Left by the coil of wire, right by French legs.' We took over from the French; the legs of one they buried in the side of the trench stick out a bit, you can't miss it."

Word Bank   dugouts   underground shelters dug by soldiers where they could rest in greater safety

Communications trenches

It was important for troops to be able to move quickly and safely into the trenches from safe areas behind the **lines**. Communications trenches (or supply trenches) ran up to the front line from these areas. Fresh troops and orders from headquarters passed through these trenches in one direction. Wounded soldiers, or soldiers due for a break, passed back along them in the other direction.

Dugouts

Sometimes soldiers could not be spared to take a break behind the lines. Then they rested in underground rooms called **dugouts** that offered some protection from bombs. The **Allies** built rough dugouts, because commanders expected the battle lines to move. The Germans built comfortable dugouts, designed for long-term use.

Sandbags

Cloth bags filled with sand or earth made an instant wall that could stop bullets. But explosions easily knocked them over, and they always needed repairing. For this reason, sandbags were mostly used where it was too damp or stony to dig.

These British soldiers are resting in a trench on the Western Front. British trenches were muddy, cold, wet, and often collapsed, burying soldiers.

↑ This German trench on the Western Front was more comfortable than the British trenches. It had rooms to sleep in and wooden floors.

Trench repairs

Pierre Jacard was an **engineer** in the French army in 1915. He was too old to be **drafted** to fight. But the army needed soldiers like him to build and repair **trenches**. In the spring of 1915, Pierre lived in the cellar of a bombed house, about 5 kilometres (3 miles) from Verdun. Every night, Pierre and his team slipped along supply trenches to the front line.

Pierre's team carried wooden beams and planks for trench repairs, and for propping up the roof inside **dugouts**. The front line trenches had a wall of sandbags in front, with thin gaps to shoot through. The gaps were held open with wooden frames, which Pierre assembled in his cellar.

French soldiers rest briefly while repairing their defences at Verdun, France, in 1916. ↓

Word Bank   artillery big guns behind the battlefront, firing shells at a long distance
draft   order someone to join the army

Different jobs

Whenever the front **line** was attacked, Pierre's crew had to work hard. The German guns would try to destroy the supply trenches behind the front line. It was Pierre's job to keep these supply routes open. Also, barbed-wire fences had to be put up in **no-man's land** after dark. At night, the sound of tapping a fence post into the ground made you an easy target. So both sides used spiral fenceposts, which screwed silently into the ground.

Pierre's team also kept **telegraph** wires working between the officers at the front, and the headquarters a few kilometres behind. The wires were constantly broken by exploding bombs, so Pierre's team had to work hard to keep communication lines open and working.

Telegraph wires were not the only way of communicating between trenches and headquarters. German troops used dogs to carry food and messages.

Bird's-eye view

Both sides sent observers up in balloons or aircraft to spy on the enemy from above. Observers helped **artillery** gunners discover how close they were to hitting distant targets. The balloon below belonged to the German army and was being used to spy on the British lines.

engineer person trained to build and mend things
telegraph simple telephone, using beeps for signals, rather than voices

LIFE IN THE TRENCHES

Peace on Earth

The leader of the Catholic Church, Pope Benedict XV, argued that Christmas was a time for peace. Germany agreed, but the other nations did not. The truces that happened in 1914 were unofficial, arranged among the soldiers, not their political leaders.

Private Bill Turner was a British soldier in the **trenches** near Ypres in Belgium. It was Christmas Day, 1914. The day before there had been fierce fighting between British and German patrols. But on Christmas morning, Turner was surprised to hear German troops singing carols. He was also shocked to see them showing their heads above their trenches – normally a sure way to get shot.

Then, one German soldier shouted "Come over here!" to the British troops. Turner and his friends thought he was joking. Turner shouted back, "No, you come here", and everyone laughed. Then a German soldier stepped up above his trench. Turner nearly shot him, but he stopped when he saw that his enemy had no gun.

These British soldiers are in a happy mood as they eat a meal to celebrate Christmas Day in a shell hole partly occupied by a soldier's grave.

Word Bank traitor someone who betrays their country, sometimes by giving information to the enemy

Brief truce

The brave German walked over to Turner's trench. He talked to Turner and some other British soldiers in English. They all agreed to call a **truce** until 4 p.m., so that both sides could go into **no-man's land** and bury their dead.

While they were in no-man's land, the enemies sang together, and played a game of soccer. Turner gave one German a tin of meat, and the German gave him tobacco to smoke. A British soldier even gave haircuts to soldiers from both armies. At 4 p.m., Turner and his friends went back to their trenches, but no-one felt like shooting for the rest of Christmas Day. The war could wait until the next morning. This friendliness between the opposing sides never happened again.

German soldiers take a break from the bitter fighting to play a game of football.

Adolf Hitler

North of Ypres, one young Austrian was very angry with the Germans who took part in the truce. He felt they were as bad as **traitors**. His name was Adolf Hitler (below right). He was a corporal in the German army during World War I. Within twenty years, he would become **dictator** of Nazi Germany.

Basic survival

William Peden was a Canadian **volunteer** who arrived in France early in 1915. His first night was spent on **sentry** duty with a British soldier. It was freezing, and Canadian food **rations** had not yet arrived, so he shared the British soldier's food. William cheered himself up one day by spoiling the enemy's lunch. While the Germans were cooking, William and his friends shot at the sandbags on the German **trench**, knocking dirt into their food.

Terrible conditions

Digging trenches (called digging-in) at Ypres in Belgium was hard for William. The ground in his part of the **line** was very wet and muddy, and already hid the bodies of thousands of dead soldiers. Even digging for a little earth to fill sandbags uncovered more bodies.

A British soldier in a water-logged trench.

Word Bank   rations   daily supplies, such as food, for each soldier

No-one could risk taking their boots off. The soldiers' feet were always wet, turning pale and wrinkly. This condition was known as **trench foot**. Serious cases could cause the skin of the foot to rot. Then there would be a serious risk of death from blood poisoning.

A lucky wound

William was "lucky". He was shot in the hand at Ypres in the spring of 1915. Wounds like this could be treated and gave a soldier the chance to get away from the horror of the trenches for hospital treatment. William was sent to the United Kingdom to recover, and survived the war. Many soldiers wished they would get a wound like William's.

Casualty

Casualties included wounded soldiers as well as dead ones. "Lucky" wounds allowed a soldier to spend a long time away from the trenches. But if a soldier was caught wounding himself to get away from the fighting, punishment was harsh: this could be two years' imprisonment with hard labour.

Food and other supplies were carried through the trenches. Feeding thousands of troops in awful conditions was very difficult.

sentry   soldier on look-out duty, watching for enemy activity
trench foot   breakdown of the skin inside wet boots, causing risk of infections

21

Digging for survival

Otto von Borries was a soldier in the German army near Serre in France in June 1916. Otto and his brothers had celebrated the start of the war. They thought it was their turn to be heroes. But now he was stuck in a muddy hole. Otto's commander wanted shelters cut deep into the side of the hill. Otto felt more like a mole than a hero. However, Otto's hole would later save his life. Although Otto didn't realize it, the Battle of the Somme was about to begin. This was to be a joint French and British attack on the German army.

At the end of June, the British **artillery** fired more than 1,500,000 **shells**, in preparation for their soldiers' attack on the German **trenches**. Otto and his friends hid in a deep **bunker** for six days.

Trench warfare survival tips

This advice was given to new soldiers arriving at the front:

- Always wear a helmet to protect your head.

- Never raise your head in the same place twice, because a **sniper** will be ready to shoot you.

- Learn to predict where a shell will land from the whistling sound it makes as it flies through the air.

- Do not light a match at night – enemy snipers will be able to target you.

- Whisper when near enemy **lines**, so the enemy won't hear where you are.

- Carry your gas mask around your neck – you won't have time to look for it if there is an attack.

Thousands of soldiers were wounded in battle. Here, Canadian troops take care of captured German soldiers wounded in September 1916.

Word Bank bunker underground shelter
machine gun gun that can fire several bullets every second

The bombardment shook the walls and blocked the entrance to their bunker. Then the guns stopped. One of the guards on duty yelled: "Get out, get out, they're coming!" Otto scrambled out, and set up his **machine gun**.

Deadly surprise

The British had stopped firing their big guns because they thought they had killed all the Germans. British soldiers stepped out into the open and walked towards the German trenches. But Otto's digging had been worth it. He and his friends had a surprise for the British – they were alive and ready to fight. Otto finally stopped shooting when he ran out of bullets. The attack was a disaster for the British: 60,000 soldiers were killed or wounded on the first day of the battle alone.

War in the air

During the preparations for the Battle of the Somme in 1916, aircraft fought for control of the skies above the battlefield. Although the **Allies** won this battle, their aircraft were not as good as modern-day planes and could not change the outcome of the war on the ground. In the photo below, mechanics of the Women's Royal Air Force (WRAF) are working on an Avro bi-plane. The WRAF was formed in 1918.

shell bullet-shaped bombs fired from a large gun
sniper hidden soldier who shoots enemy soldiers from long distances with a special gun

WAR ACROSS THE WORLD

Women and the home front

With a long war looming, men taken from factories to become soldiers had to be replaced by women. All across Europe, women became an important part of the war effort making essential arms and **ammunition** for soldiers, as they are doing in the photo below.

German plans for a quick victory against France on the **Western Front** had failed. This left Germany open to defeat from the Russian army on the **Eastern Front**, as the Germans were forced to divide their forces between the two. However, the first Russian attack in August 1914 was a disaster. Hindenburg and Ludendorff, two German commanders, surrounded and destroyed part of the Russian army at a place called Tannenberg during a fierce battle from 26 to 31 August 1914. This meant that Russia was not able to attack Germany for months while its army recovered.

Further south, Russia and **Austria-Hungary** were fighting for control of the Carpathian Mountains, on the border between the two countries. Russia's huge population provided millions of soldiers for its army. Germany and Austria-Hungary, on the other hand, had fewer soldiers, but better supplies of guns and **shells**.

This **battalion** of German soldiers is advancing on the Eastern Front in 1915.

ammunition bullets, shells, mines, and bombs
battalion large military unit made up of 300 to 1000 troops

Russians driven out!

In the summer of 1915, Germany forced the Russian army to retreat hundreds of kilometres, and took about 750,000 Russians prisoner. Russian soldiers began to lose faith in their leaders. However, Germany's success on its eastern border was not matched by its armies elsewhere in the world. Germany's few military bases overseas were soon captured by the **Allies**.

Fighting in Africa

One German commander, Colonel Paul von Lettow-Vorbeck, carried out a series of attacks against the Allies in East Africa using African troops. Another German commander, Captain Müller, and his battlecruiser *Emden*, terrorized Allied ships in the Indian Ocean, before the Australian battlecruiser HMAS *Sydney* wrecked the ship. In a series of adventures, Müller was captured but 42 other *Emden* sailors escaped being taken prisoner and returned to Germany via the **Ottoman Empire**.

Guerrilla warfare

Colonel Paul von Lettow-Vorbeck commanded German forces in East Africa. With only 3000 German and 11,000 African troops, Lettow's raiders fought a successful **guerrilla** war against Allied forces up to 150,000 strong. Lettow ended his campaign voluntarily twelve days after Germany's surrender.

The Russian army poured millions of new recruits into the Eastern Front to hold back the German advance.

Eastern Front   battlefront between Germany and Russia
guerrilla   soldier who is not part of a regular army

The Gallipoli campaign

In November 1914, the war in eastern Europe spread to include Germany's ally, the **Ottoman Empire**, which was centred in modern-day Turkey. The **Allies** needed to attack the Ottoman Empire to take the pressure off Russia which was now under attack from two sides. They decided to invade Turkey, and to capture the Dardanelles, the channel of sea that links the Mediterranean with the Black Sea. Along with the British and French, the Australia and New Zealand Army Corps (ANZACs) took part in the invasion of the area, called Gallipoli, that started on 25 April 1915.

At the British and French landings, Turkish machine gunners on the beach killed hundreds of troops. The ANZAC landings began more successfully, but ANZAC troops still did not manage to take the high ground from Turkish defenders. The invasion ground to a halt, **trenches** were dug, and casualties rose.

The man with a donkey

John Simpson, who worked as an ambulance man for the ANZAC forces, used donkeys to bring wounded men down to the beach along a dangerous path known as "**Shrapnel** Gully". After saving the lives of dozens of men, he was killed on 19 May 1915.

This photo shows Gaba Tepe in Turkey, where the Australians landed on the Gallipoli Peninsula in 1915.

Word Bank   shrapnel   sharp bits of metal from an exploding bomb or grenade

The battle is lost

In May 1915, German submarines sank some nearby Allied battleships. The surviving Allied ships had to move away, reducing the heavy gun support they had been giving their troops on the beaches. The troops were left to take care of themselves. To make matters worse, Bulgaria joined the side of Germany and the Ottoman Empire in October. This opened a new route for Germany to supply weapons to Turkey. The Turkish army would now become even harder to beat.

The Allies soon realized that they were losing the battle. The campaign had failed. In December 1915, the Allies left the area. During the course of the campaign, 10,000 ANZACs, 30,000 French and British soldiers, and as many as 80,000 Turks had been killed.

ANZAC troops charge uphill to fight Turks for control of the high ground during the Gallipoli campaign in 1915.

Gallipoli timeline

The invasion of Turkey by the Allies was called the Gallipoli campaign. Although the Allies sent thousands of soldiers, the campaign failed.

19 February 1915 – Allies bombard the coast of Turkey.

18 March – Sixteen Allied battleships attack the Turkish coast, but three ships are sunk.

25 April – ANZACs and others storm the beaches.

19 May – Turkish troops attack the Allies.

28 June – The Allies begin to make a small advance against the Turkish troops.

15 November – The Allies realize they are losing and decide to leave.

20 December – Last ANZACs leave in boats.

9 January 1916 – Last Allied troops leave Gallipoli. The campaign is over.

INDUSTRIAL WAR

These French soldiers are wearing **gas masks**, waiting for a gas attack.

Mahomet Fidale was a soldier in the French army at Ypres, on 22 April 1915. It had been a sunny, almost peaceful afternoon. No one was expecting an attack. Then, at 5 p.m., a cloud of smoke floated up from the German **trenches**. The Germans often used smoke to hide soldiers attacking, so the French thought an attack had started. Mahomet rushed to his post and began shooting.

Poison clouds

But the smoke was unusual. The cloud was green and drifted low across **no-man's land** towards Mahomet. Everyone was trying to peer through it to spot the Germans. Then as the cloud arrived, there was panic. It was not smoke – the Germans had released **chlorine** gas.

Types of poison gas

There are many types of poison gas, including:

• Tear gas – this gas feels like pepper in the eyes and throat. It is very painful but has no lasting effects.

• Mustard gas – this gas blisters the skin and eyes, causing severe pain, blindness and burns.

• Chlorine and phosgene – these gases form acid in the lungs, making them fill with body fluids. Victims literally "drown" to death.

Word Bank   chlorine   greenish-yellow gas that can kill people

Panic!

As the chlorine gas reached Mahomet, his lungs began to burn and his eyes streamed with tears. Many other soldiers had dropped their rifles and run away. But Mahomet was determined not to run and stayed in his trench. The main cloud of deadly gas blew past him and after the gas was gone he escaped. His friends had not been so lucky. Many had breathed in too much of the gas and had been killed.

Canada saves the day

The use of poison gas by the Germans was not as successful as it could have been. The Germans had not prepared enough soldiers to take full advantage of the panic. Canadian troops rushed to hold the **line**, driving the Germans back.

This famous painting by John Singer Sargent shows soldiers blinded by mustard gas.

Gas attack

Wilfred Owen was a British poet and soldier. He described how a chlorine gas attack felt in one of his poems, called *Dulce et Decorum est.* Here is an extract:

"Gas! Gas! Quick, boys! – An ecstasy of fumbling,

Fitting the clumsy helmets just in time

But someone still was yelling out and stumbling,

And flound'ring like a man in fire or lime…

Dim, through the misty panes and thick green light,

As under a green sea, I saw him drowning."

gas mask   face mask with filters to remove poison gas

An attack on Verdun

In February 1916, two German soldiers, Ernst Krieg and his brother Erich, were near Verdun in France. Their commander, Erich von Falkenhayn, had a secret plan. He guessed France would use all its reserves of soldiers to save its famous fortresses in and around the town of Verdun. If Germany kept attacking the town, France would lose hundreds of thousands of soldiers.

German guns hammered the French army for days. Ernst and Erich put cotton wool in their ears, waiting for the silence that would fall at the moment of attack. They fixed **bayonets** to the ends of their rifles, preparing to go "**over the top**". At noon on 22 February, the guns stopped. Thousands of German troops surged forwards. Ernst and Erich lost each other in the chaos. Ernst struggled through barbed wire and **mantraps**, and made it to the first French **trench**.

Battle police

After a charge began, battle police searched their own trenches for soldiers who had failed to attack. On the **Western Front**, around 1000 British and French soldiers were arrested and executed for refusing to fight.

These German soldiers on the Western Front are preparing to fire their machine guns.

Word Bank   bayonet   sharp blade fixed to a rifle, for stabbing

Surviving to fight another day

A terrified French soldier was hiding in the trench. Ernst sent him off to the German **lines**, and jumped the trench to carry on fighting. Through **machine gun** fire and **shells**, Ernst and his comrades moved forward, and captured an area defended by French troops, which was hidden in woods.

But the Germans had now gone as far as the covering fire from their **artillery** could reach. As evening came and they dug in, snow began to fall. At midnight, Ernst and Erich found each other safe, and hugged. They had both survived – at least until the fighting started again tomorrow. The battle lasted until December 1915 when France retook almost all the ground for which Erich and his comrades had fought.

> This photo shows the typical living conditions endured by French troops during the fierce fighting around Verdun in 1916.

The Battle of Verdun

The Battle of Verdun lasted from 21 February to 18 December 1916 and caused almost one million casualties.

22 February 1916 – German **infantry** take first French trenches.

6 March – French hold back new German advance at Mort Homme hill.

7 June – Germans take Fort Vaux.

July – Germans shell Fort Souville with phosgene gas.

24 October – French regain positions.

2 November – Fort Vaux retaken by France.

mantrap spring-loaded metal blades designed to snap shut on a leg when trodden on

War underground

Joseph Henry Hollow was in the 1st Australian Tunnelling Corps in 1916. Like most tunnellers, he was a bit too old to be a fighting soldier. But he was fit, strong and brave enough to tunnel.

In September 1916, Joseph was working with twelve other men at Hill 60, near Messines in France. They used spades to dig through the soggy **clay**, slowly moving underground towards the German **lines**. Some of the men dug clay from the front of the tunnel and then put it into bags to be taken away. Others took the bags back to the entrance of the tunnel. One man stayed outside the tunnel, pumping fresh air in for the rest to breathe.

Dangerous work

Tunnellers made noise as they scraped through the dirt below ground. If they were heard, enemy soldiers above could drill holes down to them and drop explosives to blow them up. Enemy tunnel crews also tried to cut wires to explosive charges.

A French tunneller tests the switch that will set off the explosives at the end of his tunnel underneath enemy positions.

Word Bank   mine   bomb left buried, or in water, to explode later when something hits it or it is set off

Destroying the Messines Ridge

Joseph's tunnel took over a year of hard work before it was finished. It reached up underneath the Messines **Ridge**, where the German army had strong defences. It was a very difficult place to attack. When all the tunnels were finished, Joseph and his team placed **mines** underneath the Germans on the ridge.

Success!

Just after 3 a.m. on 7 June 1917, the explosives went off, all at the same time. The blast woke people hundreds of kilometres away in London, and was measured by earthquake scientists in Switzerland. The German position along the ridge was destroyed. Nearly 10,000 German soldiers were killed.

> **Changing geography**
> Here, British General Herbert Plumer remembers the blowing up of 600 tonnes of explosives under the Messines Ridge in June 1917.
>
> "Gentlemen, we may not make history tomorrow, but we shall certainly change the geography."

French trench diggers come out from one of the tunnels they are digging under German lines in July 1916.

ridge long, narrow hill

The Cambrai Offensive

At 6.20 a.m. on 20 November 1917, the Germans had a nasty shock, as hundreds of tanks sent by the **Allies** drove over their **trenches**. This forced the German troops to move back for many kilometres. The attack had been ordered by the Commander of the British Forces, Sir Douglas Haig, and at first it looked as if the Allies had beaten Germany back. The attack was called the "Cambrai Offensive".

Essential support

Louis Cone was in the 11th US **Engineer** Company at Cambrai in 1917. US troops were not officially fighting yet, but during the Cambrai Offensive, Louis and his team were right behind the tanks. Their job was to help repair railway lines to keep the **artillery** supplied with guns and **ammunition**.

Cambrai timeline

The Cambrai Offensive was ordered by the Commander of British Forces, Sir Douglas Haig. He sent hundreds of tanks to force the German army back.

20 November 1917 – Allies attack, breaking the **Hindenburg Line**.

23 November 1917 – Bells ring in London to celebrate the victory.

23–28 November 1917 – Allies take Bourlon Wood, the area's most important high ground.

30 November 1917 – Germany fights back.

4 December 1917 – Allies lose all the ground gained, and more.

Word Bank   Hindenburg Line   a well-built German line of defences dug in 1916

Germany fights back

Louis was examining the train tracks at Gouzeaucourt when the Germans began to fight back on 30 November. Instead of advancing in an orderly line, German soldiers had been trained to work as small, independent teams. Each team fought alone, relying on other teams following behind to protect them from being surrounded.

Many British soldiers were almost cut off, and some generals had to scramble to escape. Over 200 Allied tanks were captured by the German advance. The **counter-attack** brought Germans into direct combat with US soldiers for the first time. Louis and his men were not armed for combat. They had to use any weapons they could find. Louis was hit in the head by **shrapnel**. But he and his men fought their way to safety.

War at sea

Neither side won the battle at sea. However, the British navy managed to block the German navy inside the North Sea, closing the gap between Britain and Norway to the north and Britain and France to the south. One large battle, at Jutland, was a draw. Britain lost more ships, but the German fleet failed to escape.

Tanks at Cambrai advance slowly towards the battlefield. On their roofs they carry bridging bundles to help the tanks cross trenches.

A coal-powered British battleship fires its guns in the heat of the Battle of Jutland, 1916.

counter-attack attempt to regain ground lost after an enemy attack

BEGINNING OF THE END

In February 1917, Germany decided that its submarines must sink any ship bringing supplies to Britain and France. German leaders knew this would kill many Americans. On 6 April 1917, the United States declared war on Germany. However, the United States was not able to fight straight away. It might take as long as a year to recruit an army, train the soldiers, make enough guns and then deliver everything to Europe. This meant that Germany still had a small chance to win the war, if it could force Britain, France, and Russia to seek peace before the United States was ready.

The Russian Revolution

Russia was the first country to leave the war. Russian soldiers created their own governing councils, called **soviets**, which voted to stop fighting. The Russian government fell to a **revolution** and, in December 1917, Russia asked Germany for peace.

Zimmerman telegram

In January 1917, British spies intercepted a message from Germany to Mexico. The "Zimmerman telegram" offered Germany's support for a Mexican invasion of the United States. The telegram convinced many Americans who had previously opposed the war that Germany was their enemy.

The United States declared war on Germany on 6 April 1917. Here a soldier says goodbye before leaving to go to war. →

Word Bank   divisions   large army formations, roughly 15,000–18,000 soldiers
morale   level of confidence and determination to succeed

Germany's last chance

With peace on the **Eastern Front,** Germany moved 42 army **divisions** to the west, to add to its 150 divisions on the **Western Front.** This gave Germany one last chance at victory – but it had to strike fast.

On 21 March 1918, Germany launched the strike. At first it was successful, causing panic among the **Allies.** But the German armies had not learned from their past mistakes and again moved too fast. Their supporting guns and supplies could not keep up with the army. In August 1918, the Allies drove the German troops back. The United States delivered its first seven combat divisions to the front line and Germany's last hope of victory was gone.

An advertisement for a war film makes a link between US soldiers and the knights of the medieval crusades.

US **artillery** fires at German trenches in September 1918.

The importance of morale

If soldiers have high **morale** and think they can win, they will fight harder. But if soldiers are tired, hungry, and feel they are losing the battle, they might refuse to carry on. The low morale of the Russian troops was one reason why they refused to carry on fighting.

soviet Russian word for "council", a small democratic group

Germany and Austria-Hungary collapse

The **Allied** armies, strengthened by fresh American troops, had broken the German defences. Soon after being driven back in August 1918, the German army began to collapse completely. The **Austro-Hungarian** Empire also began to fall apart. Yugoslavia declared its independence from the Empire on 6 October 1918. Poland announced its independence on 7 October. A Czech-Slovak republic was formed on 28 October. Austria asked for peace on 3 November.

Germany was also in chaos. The German commander, Ludendorff, resigned on 26 October. But German admirals in the navy did not want to give up and tried to force their sailors to fight one last battle. The sailors refused. They had had enough of the fighting and the war.

Thousands of German prisoners were captured by the Allies during the Second Battle of the Somme near Amiens in August 1918.

A column of German **prisoners of war** marches into captivity near Longpont in France in 1918.

Word Bank   armistice   ceasefire, or temporary halt to fighting

Rebellion

After German sailors had refused to carry on, the army also refused to continue fighting. Munich, an important German city, fell to a soldiers' rebellion on 7 November. Germany's leaders had to act fast to avoid a **revolution**. On 9 November, **Kaiser** Wilhelm II lost power in Germany. The country became a democracy, with an elected president. Friedrich Ebert was made leader. The rebel soldiers accepted Ebert's government and a revolution was prevented. The new German government agreed to peace (called the **armistice**) with the Allies on 11 November 1918. The war was over.

One track

The armistice was signed in a railway carriage parked at Compiègne, near Paris. The Allies were represented by their commander-in-chief, Marshal Ferdinand Foch (second from the right in the photograph below), and the Germans by Matthias Erzberger and other politicians. France kept the railway carriage as a symbol of its victory. Hitler used the same carriage in 1940 to accept the French surrender during World War II.

revolution   replacing a government with another one, usually by force

Some Germans did not accept Friedrich Ebert's new government. On 1 January 1919, they tried to start a **revolution** in Berlin. But the new government rounded them up with special soldiers, called *Freikorps*, and shot them.

A high cost

The war left Europe in a terrible mess. Around nine million people had been killed, and millions more were left badly injured or crippled. In Britain alone, 250,000 soldiers had lost arms or legs. The war had cost the **Allies** billions of pounds.

The Treaty of Versailles

In 1919, Germany was forced to accept the Treaty of Versailles. It was very harsh. Much of Germany's land was taken away. It was not allowed to have an airforce, and had to limit its army to 100,000 soldiers. The Allies also demanded huge amounts of money from Germany to repay the costs of fighting such a long and difficult war.

The Allies were determined to make Germany pay for the destruction the war caused in northern France and Belgium. It took many years before these ancient buildings in Ypres, Belgium, were rebuilt.

However, by 1923, Germany had fallen behind with the payments it was supposed to be making to the Allies, so France and Belgium occupied part of Germany, where coal was produced. This meant that they could take any money made from the sale of coal.

Consequences

The consequences of the war affected the rest of the 20th century. Many Germans were angry that their country had lost the war. Germany was also having to pay so much money to the Allies that the country became very poor. All this anger and poverty led to the German people electing Adolf Hitler and the Nazi Party into power in 1933. Hitler promised to make Germany strong again. His attempt to do this led directly to World War II, which began in 1939.

This is one of many graveyards in northern France where soldiers who died in World War I are buried.

Adolf Hitler inspects German troops in Nuremberg in September 1935.

TIMELINE

1914
28 June   Archduke Ferdinand is killed by a Serbian terrorist.
4 August   German troops invade Belgium.
7 August   British Expeditionary Force (BEF) lands in France.
31 August   Germany defeats Russia at the Battle of Tannenberg.
6 September   The **Allies** counter-attack at the Battle of the Marne.
15 October   A German attack is defeated at the First Battle of Ypres.

1915
22 April   Germans use chlorine gas at the Second Battle of Ypres.
25 April   Allied soldiers land on beaches at Gallipoli.
7 May   A German submarine sinks *Lusitania* passenger ship.
31 May   German zeppelin airships drop bombs on London.
4 August   Germany captures Warsaw (in modern Poland) from Russia.

1916
January   Allies end the Gallipoli campaign.
2 February   Britain introduces **drafting**, which is compulsory military service.
21 February   Battle of Verdun begins.
31 May   Battle of Jutland keeps German **fleet** trapped in the North Sea.
1 July   Battle of the Somme starts. 100,000 British troops attack at the Somme: 20,000 are killed and 40,000 are wounded in one day.

1917
31 January   Germany announces unrestricted submarine warfare against any ships helping the Allies, even **neutral** US ships.
11 March   British Army captures Baghdad from the **Ottoman Empire**.
15 March   Tsar Nicholas gives up his role as Russia's ruler.
6 April   The United States declares war on Germany.
9 April   French attack, known as the Chemin des Dames Offensive, fails.
29 April   Part of the French army mutinies.
7 June   The Allies explode huge **mines** at Messines **Ridge** to destroy the German defences.

1 July	Kerensky Offensive, the last Russian attempt to attack, fails within ten days.
31 July	British attack fails at the Third Battle of Ypres.
15 October	Mata Hari, a German spy, is executed by firing squad in France.
6 November	Revolution brings Lenin to power in Russia.
9 December	British army captures Jerusalem from the Ottoman Empire.

1918

3 March	Russia signs peace agreement with Germany.
21 March	Germany launches Operation Michael into France.
21 April	German air "ace" Baron von Richthofen is shot down over Australian **trenches**.
28 May	US army is victorious in its first major battle at the Battle of Cantigny.
15 June	Italian army defeats **Austro-Hungarian** forces at the Battle of Piave.
6 July	The United States decides to send troops to Siberia, Russia, to secure Allied interests.
16–17 July	Tsar Nicholas II of Russia, his wife, and family are killed by Russian revolutionaries.
8 August	Allies force Germany to **retreat** at the Battle of Amiens.
12 September	Second major victory for US army at the Battle of St Mihiel.
27 September	German **Hindenburg Line** broken by Allied attacks.
3 October	Germany approaches United States to seek peace terms.
23 October	Allies defeat Austro-Hungarian army at the Battle of Vittorio Veneto.
3 November	German sailors mutiny and capture port city of Kiel.
10 November	German republic is announced.
11 November	Temporary peace agreed between Allies and Germany.

1919

1 January	Berlin uprising is put down by force.
21 June	German fleet scuttles (sinks itself) at Scapa Flow, Scotland.
28 June	Treaty of Versailles is signed, ending the war.

FIND OUT MORE

Search tips

There are billions of pages on the Internet so it can be difficult to find exactly what you are looking for. These search skills will help you find useful websites more quickly:

- Use simple keywords instead of whole sentences.

- Use two to six keywords in a search, putting the most important words first.

- Be precise – only use names of people, places or things.

- If you want to find words that go together, put quote marks around them.

Books

Here are just a few of the many other books about World War I.

The Frightful First World War (*Horrible Histories*), Terry Deary (Scholastic Hippo, 2004)
Horrible Histories are fun, packed with cartoons, and this title is full of information about the war.

Remember the Lusitania!, Diana Preston (Walker & Co, 2003)
Gripping tale of three young people on the cruise ship *Lusitania*, sunk in 1915 by a German torpedo.

True Stories of World War One, Paul Dowswell & Glen Bird (Usborne, 2004)
This well written and illustrated book offers true stories from eyewitnesses.

Where Poppies Grow, Linda Granfield (Stoddart Kids, 2002)
The story of World War I told through different objects.

World War I (*Eyewitness Guides*), Simon Adams (Dorling Kindersley, 2004)
Brilliantly illustrated tour of the war, rich in facts and figures.

DVD/VHS

Films about World War I are normally aimed at an adult audience, and can be upsetting. Ask a parent or teacher before watching these.

All Quiet on the Western Front, directed by Lewis Milestone (Lionsgate/Fox, 1979, VHS)
A German boy is inspired to fight for his country, but learns that war is not glorious.

Lawrence of Arabia, directed by David Lean (Columbi Tri-Star, 1962, VHS)
A British officer joins the Arab Revolt to drive the Turkish army from Arabia.

Oh! What a Lovely War!, directed by Richard Attenborough (Paramount, 1969, VHS)
A powerful film about World War I, using words from songs sung by soldiers in the trenches.

Websites

Search tips

Most sites are aimed at adults. They can contain upsetting information or pictures. Beware! Some websites are written by people without checking their facts, and contain mistakes. Others are written by people with a particular viewpoint, which may tell only one side of a story. Books are usually more reliable as sources of factual information.

http://www.westernfrontassociation.com
A wide range of resources from amateur and professional historians.

http://www.abmc.gov
Offers web access to records of American war dead, useful for family history research.

http://www.cwgc.org
Offers web access to records of the dead of British Commonwealth countries, useful for family history research.

http://www.art-ww1.com/gb/visite.html
Original art by eyewitnesses to the Great War.

http://greatwar.nl/
An unusual web memorial, with original interviews and photography.

http://www.durandgroup.org.uk
Offers further information about underground tunnels and military mining systems during World War I.

http://www.firstworldwar.com
A great website for primary documents, with copies of telegrams, official declarations, reports, and memoirs.

http://www.awm.gov.au
The Australian War Memorial's site.

Disclaimer

Where to search

Search engine

A search engine looks through the entire web and lists all sites that match the words in the search box. It can give thousands of links, but the best matches are at the top of the list, on the first page. Try **bbc.co.uk/search**

Search directory

A search directory is like a library of websites that have been sorted by a person instead of a computer. You can search by keyword or subject and browse through the different sites like you look through books on a library shelf. A good example is **yahooligans.com**

GLOSSARY

Allies countries such as the United Kingdom, France, the United States, and Russia that fought together against Germany

ammunition bullets, shells, mines, and bombs

armistice ceasefire, or temporary halt to fighting

artillery big guns behind the battlefront, firing shells at a long distance

Austria-Hungary area in central Europe consisting of Austria, Hungary, Bohemia, and parts of Poland, Romania, Slovenia, Croatia, and Italy. It was formed in 1867 and lasted until 1918.

battalion large military unit made up of 300 to 1000 troops

bayonet sharp blade fixed to a rifle, for stabbing

British Empire group of countries formerly connected with, and controlled by, Great Britain, which was at its largest at the time of the World War I, when it included 25 per cent of the world's area

bunker underground shelter

chlorine greenish-yellow gas that can kill people

clay smooth, almost waterproof mud

counter-attack attempt to regain ground lost after an enemy attack

dictator someone who has complete power in a country

divisions large army formations, roughly 15,000–18,000 soldiers

draft order someone to join the army

dugouts underground shelters dug by soldiers where they could rest in greater safety

Eastern Front battlefront between Germany and Russia

engineer person trained to build and mend things

fleet group of warships, or an entire navy

gas mask face mask with filters to remove poison gas

guerrilla soldier who is not part of a regular army

Hindenburg Line well-built German line of defences dug in 1916

infantry foot soldiers

Kaiser name used for the rulers of Austria-Hungary and Germany

line arrangement of manned positions along a battlefront

machine gun gun that can fire several bullets every second

mantrap spring-loaded metal blades designed to snap shut on a leg when trodden on

mine bomb left buried, or in water, to explode later when something hits it or it is set off

morale level of confidence and determination to succeed

morphine strong medicine given to reduce pain

neutral not supporting either side in a war, dispute, or contest

no-man's land unclaimed area of land separating enemies

Ottoman Empire large area of southwest Asia, northeast Africa and southeast Europe controlled by an emperor. Modern-day Turkey was at the centre of the Empire.

"over the top" phrase used to describe climbing out of a trench and moving into battle

prisoner of war soldier who is captured and put in prison by the enemy during a war

rations daily supplies, such as food, for each soldier

resources useful materials, such as oil or metals

retreat move back

revolution replacing a government with another one, usually by force

ridge long, narrow hill

sentry soldier on look-out duty, watching for enemy activity

shell bullet-shaped bombs fired from a large gun

shrapnel sharp bits of metal from an exploding bomb or grenade

sniper hidden soldier who shoots enemy soldiers from long distances with a special gun

soviet Russian word for "council", a small democratic group

telegraph simple telephone, using beeps for signals rather than voices

territories areas of land belonging to one country

traitor someone who betrays their country, sometimes by giving information to the enemy

trench long, narrow hole in the ground

trench foot breakdown of the skin inside wet boots, causing risk of infections

truce temporary agreement to stop fighting

Tsar name used for the rulers of Russia

volunteer join something of one's own free will

Western Front battlefront between Germany and France

INDEX

aircraft 17, 23
armistice 38, 39
Australia 12, 13, 25, 26–27, 32
Austria-Hungary 7, 8, 9, 24, 38

balloons 17
barbed wire 11, 17, 30
battle police 30
battleships 6, 27, 35
Belgium 7, 9, 10, 18, 20, 40, 41
Britain 6, 7, 9, 10, 12, 14, 15, 18, 20, 22, 23, 26, 29, 35, 36
Bulgaria 27

Cambrai Offensive 34–35
Canada 12, 20, 22, 29
carrier pigeons 16
casualties 4, 5, 21, 22, 26, 27, 40
chlorine gas 28, 29
Christmas Day, 1914 18–19
communications 15, 16, 17
costs of war 40–41

dugouts 14, 15, 16

East Africa 25
Eastern Front 24, 25, 37
executions 30

Ferdinand, Archduke Franz 8
fire step 14
flanking 10
Foch, General Ferdinand 39
food 20, 21
France 4, 6, 7, 8, 9, 10, 11, 14, 16, 20, 22, 24, 25, 26, 28, 30–31, 32, 33, 36, 37, 38, 39, 41

Gallipoli 13, 26–27
gas 5, 22, 28–29
Germany 6, 7, 9, 10, 11, 12, 13, 14, 17, 18, 19, 22, 23, 24, 25, 27, 28, 29, 30, 33, 34, 35

defeat 36–39
repayment of war costs 40–41
"Great Game, the" 6
guerilla warfare 25

Haig, Sir Douglas 13, 34
Hindenburg, General Paul von 24
Hitler, Adolf 19, 39, 41

India 12

Japan 9
Jutland 35

Kaiser Wilhelm II 8, 9, 39

Ludendorff, General Erich 24, 38

mantraps 30, 31
Marne, Battle of the 11
Messines Ridge 33
mines 32, 33
morale 36, 37
mustard gas 28, 29

New Zealand 11, 12, 26–27
no-man's land 4, 5, 11, 17, 19, 28

Ottoman Empire 12, 13, 25, 26–27
"over the top" 4, 5, 30
Owen, Wilfred 29

phosgene gas 28, 31
Plumer, General Herbert 33
poison gas 5, 28–29
Poland 38
Princip, Gavril 8
prisoners of war 25, 38

reasons for war 8
revolution 36, 39, 40
Russia 6, 7, 8, 9, 24, 25, 26, 36, 37

sandbags 14, 15, 16, 20
Schlieffen Plan 9–10
Serbia 8
Somme
    First Battle of the 22–23
    Second Battle of the 38
South Africa 12
spying 17
submarines 27, 36
supply trenches 15, 16, 17
survival tips 22

tanks 34, 35
tear gas 28
telegraph 17
Treaty of Versailles 40
trenches 4, 5, 11, 12, 18, 19, 22, 23, 34
    communications/supply trenches 15, 16, 17
    design of 14, 15
    digging 11, 20, 22, 26, 31
    repairs 16
trench foot 21
truces 18, 19
tunnels 32–33
Turkey see Ottoman Empire

United States, the 9, 34, 35, 36, 37, 38

Verdun 14, 16
    Battle of 30–31

war graves 41
Western Front 10, 11, 14, 15, 24, 30, 37
women 23, 24
Women's Royal Air Force (WRAF) 23
wounds 21
    see also casualties

Ypres 18, 19, 20, 21, 28, 40
Yugoslavia 38

Zimmerman telegram 36